From
Father to Son

From Father to Son

Wisdom for the Next Generation

— Allen Appel —

St. Martin's Press   New York

FROM FATHER TO SON. Copyright © 1993 by Allen Appel. All rights reserved. Printed in the United States of America. No part of this book may be used or reproduced in any manner whatsoever without written permission except in the case of brief quotations embodied in critical articles or reviews. For information, address St. Martin's Press, 175 Fifth Avenue, New York, N.Y. 10010.

Editor: Jared Kieling
Production Editor: David Stanford Burr
Design: Basha Zapatka

**Library of Congress
Cataloging-in-Publication Data**

Appel, Allen.
      From father to son : wisdom for the next generation / Allen Appel.
                    p.   cm.
            ISBN 0-312-09814-6
            1. Fathers—Quotations, maxims, etc.
      2. Quotations, English.   I. Title.
      PN6084.F3A67   1993
      306.874′2—dc20   93-25958
                                          CIP

10   9   8   7   6

For my father, Allen R. Appel, Jr.
1911–1992
For all of the advice, all of the help,
all of the years

━ INTRODUCTION ━

Memory. Standing on a box, leaning against the rough wooden workbench. My father starts an eight-penny nail into a block of soft pine. I am four, maybe five. He hands me the hammer. Not a toy, but a heavy, honest-to-God tool. His hammer. *Go ahead*, he says.

I swing at the nail with a boy's love of hitting, miss the nail, try again, tap, tap, getting nowhere, look up at him.

He takes my hand and slides it down the handle.

Like this, he says, gently. *Don't choke up on it. Let the tool do the work.* Together we strike swift hard strokes and I feel the steel nail thunk into the soft wood—solid, pleasing. *That's right*, he says. *That's good.*

Don't choke up on it. Let the tool do the work.

I grew up in West Virginia in the 1950s. The fathers kept the sons in hand and passed along information, advice, rules to live your life by. A quick phrase, often humorous, simple enough to remember over the years. Now, a middle-aged man, I realize how lucky I was to receive this wisdom. So I asked my friends, friends of friends, strangers, to help me remember our fathers and what they taught us so we could gather it and pass it along. This book is the result.

Read it. Remember. Write in it. Give it away. To your father, perhaps, to see what he remembers. To your son, perhaps, to help him grow. Because you love him.

We live in hard times. Boys need all the help they can get.

Let's tell them what we know.

—ALLEN APPEL

From
Father to Son

~ WORK ~

If you want to make sure that a job is done badly, pay for the whole thing in advance.

Before you start a project, think hard on how you want it to end.

It doesn't matter how strong you are, if you lift something in the wrong way you're going to hurt yourself. Keep your legs together, your hands on the inside, and bend your knees.

*F*or a worker, the week has seven to-days. For the lazy man, it has seven tomorrows.

If someone says he'll get back to you later, ask him when. And get his name.

You don't need a lot of fancy equipment to be a writer. Remember that Abraham Lincoln wrote the Gettysburg Address on the back of an envelope while on the train to Gettysburg.

My daddy used to tell a story his dad told him. Two horses were pulling a cart. One horse was barely leaning against the traces, the other was pulling for all he was worth. The driver was whaling away at the horse who was giving all he had. A bystander asked, "Why don't you beat the other horse?" The driver replied, "Don't you know? You always beat the horse that pulls." See, everybody piles the biggest load on the willing horse.

—DAVID JONES

*T*ouch a piece of paper only once. A busy man will get more done by either tossing a piece of paper into the trash can or sending it on its way with the appropriate action.

Waste an hour in the morning and you'll spend all day trying to catch it up.

The best time to answer your mail is as soon as you've read it.

$\mathcal{T}$he four B's of creativity are Bed, Bath, Beach, and Bus. These are the places that ideas come to you, where solutions occur. They can pop into your head as if by magic, so be prepared to grab them. Never go to bed without a pen and paper nearby, and no matter how convinced you are that you'll remember it in the morning, make yourself get up and write the idea down.

*I*t's not enough to have an idea, even if it's a great idea. You've got to do the work to implement it. That's the hard part.

If you really want to know what a fellow is like, give him some authority and see what he does with it.

An hour's work done in the morning is worth two done in the evening.

The reverse side has its own reverse side. If you've got a job to do, turn it over in your mind and look at it from all angles before you make any important decisions.

Think ahead and plan for all eventualities. The cow doesn't miss her tail until fly time.

If you try and fail, try again. If you fail again, contract the job out.

*L*earn to type.

One volunteer is worth five hired hands.

Get a job.

If you've got a trade, you've got a job.

If you can't make it in America, you can't make it anywhere.

My step-grandfather had been an oil man back in West Virginia in the boom days. He said when you were up on a rig and it started to fall you never jumped off. He had a wooden leg earned learning that hard lesson. When she starts to fall, he said, ride her to the ground. It's a pretty good lesson, even though I don't think I'll be climbing many oil derricks.

Never jump off, hang on, ride her to the ground.

—ALLEN APPEL

~ CARS ~

Y ou can always take a curve ten miles an hour faster than the sign says.

Brake before you get into the curve, accelerate through it.

If a cop stops you, don't get out of your car unless he tells you to do so. Uncalled for jumping out of cars makes a cop very nervous.

*I*t's usually better to have a drunk driver in front of you where you can watch him.

Don't buy a used car, you're just buying someone else's problems.

Don't expect that buying a car, new or used, is going to be a rational experience. Be as knowledgeable as you can when you go into it, but generally it's just two fools agreeing on a price.

The only guy you have to watch out for is the guy in front of the guy behind you.

My father had a heart attack and was in intensive care. He motioned me over to the bedside. "Allan," he said, his voice as thin as paper, "take the car in for an oil change. But make sure you tell them to give you the old filter. If they don't give you the old filter, they just wipe it off and put it right back on."

—ALLAN JANUS

TOOLS, WOOD-WORKING, AND REPAIRS

*L*et the tool do the work.

If you want the job done right, do it yourself.

Do things right. You will never remember how much time it required once you're finished.

*T*here are only two ways to do a job: the right way, and any other way.

If you don't have the time to do it right, when will you have the time to do it over?

Never break one thing to fix another.

Measure twice: Cut once.

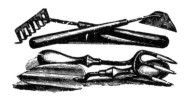

*L*earn to use your tools: A good carpenter can build an entire house using only a carpenter's square for measuring and figuring.

When using a handsaw, remember that the blade cuts only on the forward thrust.

Well begun is half done.

$\mathcal{F}$inish what you start.

Use two hands.

Getting the right tool is half the job.

The right tool will make a hard job simple, the wrong tool will make a simple job hard.

In any craft you wish to master, buy one excellent tool.

*W*hen painting, everything takes two coats. No matter what it says on the paint can.

Build something as if you want it to last forever—or at least long after you are gone. If you do, and it does, it's a reminder of your time on this earth.

$\mathcal{H}$old the hammer at the end of the handle, don't choke up.

Drive every nail as if it were the only one you'll ever drive—and a hundred carpenters are watching.

Any home-repair job will entail at least three trips to the hardware store.

$\mathcal{P}$ut the top back on.

When you take apart something complex, lay the pieces out in the order they were removed; if *very* complex, draw a sketch of how it came apart.

Never force anything that's stuck. Stop and think it over. There's a gentle way to get it unstuck.

*I*f you're working with a screwdriver or any threaded object, remember the rhyme—Righty Tighty, Lefty Loosey. Turn the screw or nut to the right, it gets tighter; turn it to the left and it loosens.

Never cut what you can untie.

The third half hitch is always a waste of time. (The first two knots will do the job.)

*T*he best carpenter makes the smallest pile of sawdust.

My father was "Mr. Fixit." I never remember seeing a repairman at our house when anything went on the fritz. Later, as I got older, I figured out that the reason we never had anyone else fix things is that we couldn't afford to. Our television set was always kind-of-working. My dad worked on it continually.

—LLOYD GREENBURG

My dad had a great appreciation of humor, loved to joke and talk with his buddies, and was a colorful character. He never repaired appliances in his life, and I, of course, assumed that real men did not fix appliances. This was a problem the first few years of my marriage to someone whose father was an electrical engineer and not only fixed everything in their house, but then scoured the neighborhood for additional repairs.

—JOHN MCGUIRE

MANNERS
~ AND ~
DEPORTMENT

*F*irst impressions go a long way and last a long time.

Never whine: The squeaky wheel doesn't get the grease these days, it gets replaced.

Pay attention to everyone. Even a fool can sometimes give good advice.

. . . .

Never let yourself be flattered by the words and smiles of your enemies.

Develop a firm handshake, which shows character. A weak handshake reflects insecurity. And always look a man in the eye when you're shaking hands with him.

Never call another man by his first name until he tells you it's all right to do so.

Any man more than ten years older than you are is called Mister.

Don't let people take your picture standing around with your hands in your pockets or a drink in your hand. You'll look like a bum.

*T*ell the truth. You'll go to hell for lying the same as stealing.

Listen to the other guy when you're having a conversation. Too many people spend the other fellow's talking time deciding what they're going to say.

A liar and a thief are the lowest form of human life. Generally, they are one and the same.

*A*lways date your letters.

When you sit down at a table, put your napkin in your lap. Nobody is exactly certain what to do after that.

Don't believe rumors. One dog barks because it's seen something, every other dog in the neighborhood barks because it heard the first dog bark.

*I*f you think you may be wrong, it's time to reconsider your position.

If you borrow something, make sure you return it in at least as good or better condition than you got it. And if it runs on gasoline, return it with a full tank.

Do everything as if it were an advertisement of your abilities. It is.

My father taught me to be honest, to do the best job I could do, and to be fair to whomever I was dealing with. Whenever I worked for anyone, he always insisted I see the job through. He would not let me quit until the job was finished. He taught me good manners and how to be a gentleman. After twenty-five years of marriage, I still hold the door for my wife.

—HARRY STEELE

*W*hen I was fourteen years old there was a girl in our school who was ridiculed for her looks. She was not really bad-looking, but, like most budding adolescents, I wanted to be part of the gang. One day my old man caught me joking about Kathy's appearance, and startled my brother and myself by insisting that I apologize to her on the spot. When I replied that Kathy was not there, he did not let that technicality get in the way, but told me to simply pretend that she was, and to say I was sorry. It wasn't easy, but I did it, and learned a powerful lesson from the experience.

—TONY ROHLING

~ MONEY ~

Give a decent wage. If you pay peanuts, you get monkeys.

There are lots of ways to get rich, but the easiest way is to manage other people's money.

If you want to be rich, make something that works for you while you're asleep.

*I*f something seems to be a real good bargain, think twice. There's probably a reason for it. Best to find out what that reason is.

No matter how you try to rationalize it, if you buy stolen goods you're just as bad as the original thief.

Don't fall into the trap of "book value." The worth of a thing is what someone will pay for it.

*J*f you *have* to borrow money, always ask for a lot more than you need, and always wear your suit when you've got your hand out.

Before you borrow money from a friend, decide which you want more; the friend or the money. And before you *loan* money to a friend, decide which you want to keep.

Don't loan anyone more money than you can afford to lose.

$\mathcal{P}$ay what you owe, and pay it as quickly as you can.

Sometimes you've got to spend your money. Stop saving everything for that rainy day. Ever see an armored truck following a hearse?

We were very poor, so my father worked two jobs at a time, sometimes three. So he wasn't home that much. On Christmas morning we would have to wait upstairs while he finished his milk deliveries before going down to open our presents. But he was a sweet man, very loving. He took the time to do things with his kids. I think he taught by example, rather than by direct advice.

—SAM WYNKOOP

_M_y father always used to say, "Money talks and everything else walks." Ironically, he was a printer by trade and earned his living for thirty years by printing money at the Bureau of Engraving and Printing. I don't really think his job had much to do with his philosophical position. I just think he felt that was the way the world worked. And as money becomes more of a necessity in my own life, I am beginning to see more of what he was talking about.

—FRANK DiPerna

*D*ad often said, "A man that doesn't pick up a penny that's laying on the ground won't ever amount to much." And if I'm not mistaken, the statement was prefaced by, "I remember my dad always saying . . ." So I'm the third (at least) generation to have received this wisdom.

—RIC ANDERSON

~ SPORT ~

If you're going to play any game well, first of all you need to learn to run.

If you don't pay attention, you're going to get hurt.

Always assume the gun is loaded.

*W*e had just won a basketball game, and the roar of the crowd was still ringing in my ears. The coach looked at me and said, "You know, if you had missed the shot, they all would have thought you were a bum." Good advice. I never forgot it.

—JOHN LALLY

To break in your baseball glove, rub it with neat's-foot oil, put a ball in the pocket, and wrap twine around the glove. Sleep with it under your pillow every night for two weeks.

Reef your sail when you first think of it.

On the water, (in boats) things go wrong very quickly.

I picked this up from an old baseball coach: *Don't throw the ball more than you need to.* The more often you throw it, the more often someone has to catch it, increasing the chance of errors at either end. This is more than just baseball wisdom, it applies to everything that a person can do. In any project, you can minimize mistakes by eliminating unnecessary actions.

—GEOFF FULLER

━ WOMEN, WIVES, AND FAMILY ━

*I*f you can't bring her home in the daylight, don't take her out at night.

If you want to win the daughter, start with the mother.

There's more to marriage than four bare legs in a bed.

Never marry a woman with a weak father.

Marriage is a 70/30 proposition. Expect to give 70 percent to get 30 percent.

It doesn't help *you* if her half of the boat sinks.

*F*amily members are responsible for each other: Look out for your little brother, look out for your little sister.

Never let anyone say anything bad about your mother.

The biggest thing a man learns from children is patience.

⏤ COOKING AND DRINKING ⏤

Learn to cook; for yourself, for your family, for your friends. There are plenty of books that will tell you everything you need to know.

You can't have too much garlic.

Never tell anyone what you put into your sausage.

When boiling vegetables, things that grow above the ground go into water *after* it begins to boil. Things that grow below the ground go into the pot when the water is cold.

Never buy good bread already sliced.

The worst homemade biscuit is better than the best store-bought biscuit.

One should be able to see the back of the refrigerator when you open the door.

Helping the cook is a way of showing love, and it doesn't hurt when it comes to seconds.

Stir from the bottom up.

A glutton digs his own grave with his own teeth.

Never go grocery shopping when you're hungry.

Always eat your steaks rare, and drink your whiskey straight.

*T*he smallest peppers are the hottest.

If you put yellow mustard on a pretzel it tastes exactly like ballpark hot dogs. This makes a good bar bet.

If you can't do it when you're sober, don't say it when you're drunk.

Never drink if you've got work to do.

Never drink when you're alone.

Never drink while the sun is shining.

~ DRESS ~

Always buy silk neckties and don't worry if when you wear them they're slightly wrinkled. A tie that is perfectly flat is almost always made out of something that is not silk. Also, never have your ties dry-cleaned, they come back perfectly flat.

A winter coat unbuttoned is no coat at all.

Never buy mail-order shoes.

*W*hen you're dressed up, always carry a handkerchief even if you don't see anyone doing it anymore. They come in handy more often than you might suppose.

Wear the same type (but not as expensive) of clothes as your boss. Unless your boss is a woman.

Pack light, travel light.

~ FIGHTING ~

*I*f someone wants to fight you, never step outside. Do your fighting right where you are.

Never get into a fight with a man who has nothing to lose.

Never hit anyone with your hand. Hit him with *something*, the heavier the better.

*I*f it looks like you're going to have trouble or a fight and you can't get out of it, better to go at it right now.

If a fight looks inevitable, throw the first punch. The first punch is quite often the last.

All bullies are cowards, and most cowards are bullies.

Keep punching.

~ MILITARY ~

*E*nthusiasm is contagious. So is excitement and panic. Beware!

In war, the only bullets that count are the ones that hit.

When you demand the impossible, don't be surprised at what you get.

From my old platoon sergeant, Staff Sergeant Quinell Hayes, when asked if we needed to pack extra boots, socks, etc., in our packs when going to the field (thereby increasing the weight of the packs). His answer was always the same: It's better to have it and not need it, than need it and not have it.

—CRAIG ROBERTS

*T*ake care of your equipment before you take care of yourself.

The more you sweat in peace, the less you bleed in war.

They say an army travels on its stomach. The truth is, an army travels on its feet. Take care of your boots.

Know the rule book in peacetime. Throw it out in war.

Never ask a man to do what you wouldn't do.

It's easier to pull a chain than push one.

An amateur thinks tactics. A professional thinks logistics.

*T*here's no such thing as a "flesh wound."

If the enemy is in range, so are you.

When in doubt, empty your magazine.

The important things are always simple.

The simple things are always hard.

*T*he easy way is always mined.

If it's stupid but it works, it ain't stupid.

Never share a foxhole with anyone braver than you are.

Teamwork is essential, it gives the enemy other people to shoot at.

~ ADVICE ~

There're two important things to remember about advice: 1. It's free, and 2. You don't have to take it.

A good example is the best sort of advice.

Giving someone well-intentioned advice after they've made some mistake is like giving medicine to a corpse. Even if it's the right sort of medicine it isn't going to do a bit of good.

· ·

Good advice can be real annoying if the problem is already past fixing.

If someone who loves you gives you advice, you ought to consider it pretty seriously, even if you don't like it.

Most people who are asking for advice are really asking for encouragement. There's nothing wrong with that. Unless it's stupid or illegal, go ahead and encourage them.

~ TRUTH ~

*H*onesty without charity is mistaking the idol for the God.

A lie that is part truth is harder to fight than an all-out lie.

You can't do any better than to tell the truth. Remember that a liar is the beginning of a thief.

*T*he man who lied yesterday isn't going to be believed tomorrow.

Don't trust a man who will lie for you. He'll just as easily lie *to* you.

Love the truth.

~LIFE~

Do the best you can, and let the rough edge drag.

Remember, there's a lot of injustice in this world. Some of it is going to come your way.

A guilty conscience usually hurts worse than the punishment you'll probably get. Or at least it ought to.

. . . .

It doesn't hurt to pray for miracles, but I wouldn't waste much time on it. Save the prayers for thank-you's.

Bad news travels the same speed, usually fast, whether it's true or not. Often it's best to let bad news cool a bit before you act on it.

Don't set the trap in sight of the rabbit.

*B*etter to make sure that you're buying a good dog rather than a dog of a good kind. This applies to any kind of animal and more than a few life situations. Unless you're in it for the money, pedigrees don't have much practical applications.

It's an old legal maxim that says every dog is allowed one bite. That applies to people as well. Every man deserves a second chance.

It's easy to find a stick to beat a dog.

When a chicken crosses a road, it ain't to get to the other side. It's because your fences need mending.

The shortest path between two points is a straight line. But often the *best* path is one that touches all the bases.

If you race through life, you're just going to get to heaven in a sweat.

The distance between 0 percent and 95 percent is just about the same as the distance between 95 percent and 100 percent as far as effort is concerned. Everything gets harder at the end, but you have to push when you're in the home stretch.

Without question, enthusiasm is the single most important quality in a successful man.

If you can't be good at something, at least be enthusiastic.

*E*ven bad teachers learn more than they teach by teaching. Good teachers teach to learn. The Chinese have a saying: Teaching is learning twice.

One day with a great teacher can often beat a year of study or a hundred books.

$\mathcal{M}$y father taught me to read from one of those first-grade readers. "Oh my," said Dick. "See Spot run." My father reacted right away, taking a bright red pencil, crossing out the "Oh my's" and writing in "Odds bodkins," "Gadzooks," "Gorblimey," and such all down the page. It was a revelation. It was the opposite of boring. The possibilities seemed endless and wonderful and I think it was at that moment I became a writer.

—GORDON CHAPLIN

*S*uccess is based on personal values: humility, integrity, honesty, simplicity, responsibility, and authenticity. It has nothing to do with money or status.

The absolute rule is the best sort of rule. It's the easiest to explain, and the easiest to enforce.

The older you get, the better I'm gonna look.

A pig doesn't get fat by being weighed.

You can't tell the depth of the well by the length of the handle on the pump.

Fix the problem, not the blame.

Everybody wants to go to heaven, nobody wants to die to get there.

Know where you're going, always be aware of where you are, and never forget where you came from.

If you try and fail, try again. If you fail again, redefine success.

Be on time. A person who is habitually late is seen as a special species of self-important fool.

Don't write checks with your mouth that your butt can't cash.

_C_an't never did anything.

The number of books on your shelf won't impress an intelligent person. It's the quality of books that count.

When you're out in the desert, it doesn't pay to be particular about the sort of water that's available.

The tadpole doesn't think he's going to end up a frog, he dreams of becoming a whale.

*I*t's okay to stumble if you catch yourself, what you're trying to avoid is the fall. In fact, if you're halfway into a bad spot, most people will give you a lot of credit for getting yourself out, even if it was your own fault getting in there in the first place.

When you fall down into a deep hole, either one of two things are going to happen: You're going to get out, or you're going to die.

*J*ust because it looks good at night, doesn't mean it's going to look good in the daylight. And in fact, the opposite is almost always true.

The price of a man's hat has got nothing to do with the size and quality of his brain.

If you give a pig flowers to smell, it's just going to eat them.

Even the best song gets irksome if you hear it often enough.

Practice.

If you're willing, you're able.

A fool is still a fool, even if he drives a big car.

Always throw your hat over the wall. That way you're going to *have* to climb the wall.

If you put too much of anything in your bag, eventually it's going to break.

*W*here there's smoke, there was fire at least once upon a time.

Going too far is just as bad as coming up short.

All the money in the world won't buy back one lost minute.

Even the best writer has to erase.

Just because the water's deeper doesn't necessarily mean the fish are going to be any bigger.

*I*f you spend all your time looking out for snakes, you're going to miss the scorpion.

There's always a snake in Paradise.

It's less work to keep a good reputation than it is to get it back once you've lost it.

If you don't take the pill, don't expect the medicine to work.

Rich people have problems too; it's just that no one feels sorry for them.

No one can take away your good name. Be careful that you don't give it away.

Being a hero is hanging on for one minute longer.

You're never going to cure fear by taking medicine out of any kind of a bottle.

Don't call the alligator a bad name until you're already across the river.

*J*ust because a boy doesn't look like his father doesn't mean he isn't the man's son.

Always getting ready to do something is just the same as never having done it.

When someone gives you a balloon, don't ask the giver to blow it up.

If you believe something is impossible, it will be.

It isn't as hard to study as it is to be stupid.

*I*t doesn't do you any good to run if you're headed down the wrong road.

Watch the ounces and the pounds will take care of themselves.

It's not enough to know how to ride, you've got to know how to fall.

Be yourself.

Don't spend your time worrying about things you can't do anything about.

The true way to end up looking like a fool is to pretend you know something that you don't.

Get it on paper.

My dad, who was an architect, always said: If it intrudes, hide it; if it still intrudes, make it sensitive; if it *still* intrudes, paint it red. I've applied this advice to a wide range of situations.

*D*on't listen to other people's secrets.

Work hard to get what you want, then take the time to enjoy it.

I can't recall my father ever striking me. Probably the worst thing for me would have been for Dad to tell me that I had really disappointed him (I can't recall him ever saying that either). I love Dad very, very much and am saddened that I am on the other side of the country where I can't help him out.

—LARRY NEMECEK

Never get a tattoo, you'll be sorry later on. Guaranteed.

A lot of people have said that God is on the side with the biggest battalions. My dad pointed out that it would increase my odds of coming out of a fight with my skin intact if I were on that side as well.

Be patient and endure. The longest day has the shortest night.

Make up your mind one way or the other. If you try to sit between two seats, you're going to end up on the ground. And if you try to chase two rabbits, you're not going to catch either one of them.

Don't stop trying your hardest and doing your best until a thing is really finished. It's stupid to swallow the whole cow and then choke on the tail.

Three people can keep a secret as long as two of them are dead.

*J*f you're going to eat with the devil, you'd better have a long spoon.

Don't think you can get away with something forever. The mills of God grind slowly, but they grind exceedingly small.

If you don't make mistakes, you're not going to make anything.

Dejazmatch (equivalent to General) Abai Kassa, my father, is not exposed to western education system. He and other patriots in Ethiopia fought the Mussolini's forces as guerrillas for five years (1936–1941). He taught me endurance, patience, resistance, flexibility, open-mindedness, compassion, integrity, and discipline.

—HAILEMARIAM ABAI

Respect your religion and elders.

Fight for your country.

One who starts fighting suffers the consequence of starting that fight.

Fathers love to catch their children doing something right.

Listen when somebody speaks to you before you answer.

Work for self-esteem and self-discipline.

When arguers come at you to argue, remind yourself not to say yes or no.

Do not depend on the help of others.

Never give up on anything you want to do.

—HAILEMARIAM ABAI

*I*n order to live a good and clean life my father has taught me six basic rules:

If I don't do it, then you don't do it.

No one knows the truth but your conscience and God.

You are never a failure as long as you give it your best.

Do not forget your culture.

Do not do something just because I am around.

Education and honesty are two of the most important things you should have.

—DAGEM HAILEMARIAM

*D*on't be surprised at the strange things you're going to see in life. A pig may whistle, even if he doesn't have the mouth for it.

When two people ride the same horse at the same time, one of them has to ride behind the other.

Raindrops can't tell jeans from leather.

Don't think that just because a man gets old he might not be dangerous. The wolf may lose his teeth, but not his inclination.

Never try to put a saddle on an eel.

*I*t's not very satisfactory to scratch your shoe when your foot itches.

Sometimes danger comes in small packages. Even though a needle isn't very big, you wouldn't want to swallow one.

Don't be contemptuous of anything, and don't get too big for your britches. The man who spits into the wind spits into his own face.

Once you've made up your mind to do something, do it as soon as possible.

No matter how far you've gone, if you realize you're on the wrong road, turn back.

If you have to kill a snake, kill it once and for all.

Don't make gratitude the price of charity.

*A*lways try to put in an appearance, especially if something has gone wrong. If you're not going to be there when they're passing out the blame, it's likely going to end up being your fault.

There are two things it doesn't do a lick of good to be angry about: Things you can do something about, and things you *can't* do something about. Either fix it, or forget it.

Death is a dying man's friend.

*I*t's a fact of life that sometimes the worst hog will get the best apple. It may not be fair but that's the way it is.

Envying what another man has never made any man rich.

Never make a fool out of yourself just to make other people laugh.

It isn't a bad idea to have friends in both heaven and hell.

*A*nything another man has done, you can do.

If everyone took care of himself, everyone would be taken care of.

$\mathcal{B}$efore you buy a house, go knock on the neighbor's door.

Never live next door to a river or a lawyer.

A good archer is not known for his arrows, but his aim.

$\mathcal{D}$on't hide anything from your preacher, your doctor, or your lawyer.

If something is worth doing, there's always going to be some risk involved. Seize the day.

Try to consider what happens after what happens next.

*M*y father was as compulsive and efficient as I am. At Saturday morning breakfast, he would give each of us a list of chores that we had to get done for the day before any free time. My mother would get very upset when she got a list.

—DAVID FISSEL

*W*hat's important are the processes of life, the pursuit of goals rather than their attainment. You won't believe it when you're young, but try to keep it in mind, at least it will ease some of the pain.

Mistakes can be important even though it doesn't seem that way. We learn from recognizing errors.

The trip is always short and easy for the guy who's giving directions.

*L*ife is a series of obligations. Accept them with good grace. If you spend all your time trying to duck your responsibilities, you'll die an unhappy man.

What a braggart goes on about having the most of is usually just those areas where he is most deficient.

Some people are always going to say bad things about you. What you want to do is live your life so no one will believe them.

Never cut someone else down just to build yourself up.

If you have to do something you're afraid of, be the first in line to face it.

Never give up.

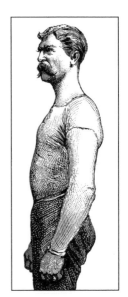

*L*augh at what you're afraid of. Wrestle it to the ground.

If you have books but don't read them, or don't use your public library, you're no better off than a man who can't read.

The best steel is forged by going through the hottest fire and being beaten the longest.

Saying bad things about other people is a cheap way to make yourself look better.

*P*eople who ask for truly honest criticism are almost always asking for praise.

Don't be so positive of your own morality. Eating human flesh is a virtue in cannibal country.

Just because everyone in the country is saying something stupid, doesn't mean it isn't stupid.

*J*f you're going to take the lead, you've got to expect to take some heat. They say you can tell which men were the pioneers by the arrows in their backs.

It's just as bad to doubt everything as it is to believe it.

Even a good man is going to pick up a little dirt sometime.

If you're always depending on other people, you're always going to be disappointed.

Don't judge a man's character by the size of the Bible he carries.

*M*y father, who was in politics, told me to remain a bit mysterious. A good friend and father figure to him gave him this advice. It makes people wonder about you, draws them to you as we are all drawn to a mystery.

—JOE MILLS

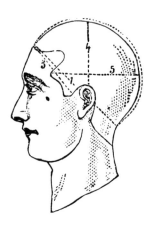

*I*f you want to know what's on the road ahead, ask someone who's coming back.

It's the word "yes" that gets you in trouble. "No" hardly ever causes harm.

Don't go to skinning the bear before you've drug him out of the hole.

Simplify.

You row with whatever oar is in the boat.

Just because the dog is licking your hand right now doesn't mean he isn't going to bite you later.

For every action there is a reaction. Everything you do or say has consequences. Don't let this fact slow you down, but be aware of it.

$\mathcal{A}$dvice from my maternal grandfather, Lloyd Wolf. He worked for the city of Huntington Park as a metal worker and welder and even built its first jail. When I was seven years old, he locked me in one of the jail cells and left me there alone for about an hour. When he came back, he asked me if I liked it. Of course I didn't. He said, "Then never break the law. If you do, you'll wind up in one of these." I think that's the reason I became a cop. Insurance.

—CRAIG ROBERTS

*I*t's hard to keep in mind, but a beautiful woman is not necessarily a good woman or the best woman for you.

You'll be amazed at how many people can have absolutely ridiculous or immoral beliefs and still get through the day without any problems. Don't try to enlighten them, they're doing fine without your help.

$\mathcal{I}$f you are going to try to write or create something really original, don't talk about it before you start.

Don't take yourself too seriously.

The harder you work, the luckier you get.

On Good Friday when I was nine, he got sick. On Easter Sunday, he went to the hospital. The next night, he died. He will always be youthful, handsome, and riding his horse. And I will have to grow old for both of us.

—NEAL POINTER

~ ACKNOWLEDG-MENTS ~

I would like to thank the following sons and fathers who replied to my questions with stories and comments about themselves, their fathers, and their own children. During the course of this project I received fascinating and moving letters virtually every day, and they are still coming in. If any readers would like to contribute to future books on fathers and advice, you can write to me care of Jared Kieling, my fine editor at St. Martin's Press, 175 Fifth Ave., New York, New York 10010.

Hailemariam Abai
Henry Allen
Ric Anderson
Allen R. Appel, Jr.
David Appel
Clifford Arnebeck
Bob Arnebeck
Ed Barton
Burkey Belser
Larry Bridge
Gordon Chaplin

John William Cody
Leo J. Conway
Fred L. Davis
Lloyd Davis
Frank DiPerna
Carl E.
Don Fear
Paul Feinberg
Francis Fisher
David Fissel
Thomas E. Fissel

Michael Foster
Geoff Fuller
Bill Garrison
David Greenberg
Lloyd Greenberg
Marvin Jay
  Greenberg
Dagem
  Hailemariam
Quinell Hayes
Coit Hendley
Frank Herrera
Charlie Himes
Allan Janus
Bill Jones
Larry Kahaner
Max Kahaner
Carl Kalish
Dejazmatch
  Abai Kassa
John Lally
Ned Leavitt
Perry Letson
Brian McCall
Charles Brandon
  (Brady) McGuire

John McGuire
Ed McNamara
James McPherson
Earl Merkl
Larry Merkl
Joe Mills
Luthor Morris
Bob Nichols
Joe (Lumir Joseph)
  Nemecek
Larry Nemecek
Frank Peteroy
Homer Pointer, Sr.
Neal Pointer
Mark Power
T. R.
Tim Ridgely
Craig Roberts
William Floyd
  Roberts, Sr.
Joseph Rohling
Tony Rohling
Arthur Rosenthal
Bernard Rosenthal
Terry Scott
Donald Shelton

Ralph Staiger
Albert Steele
Harry Steele
Bhob Stewart
Joe B. Stewart
Ray Stewart
Robert Marion
  Stewart
Vladimir
  Toumanoff

Clement Laird
  Vallandigham
Sam Walton
Harold G. Watkins
A. Emerson Weins
Kenton Weins
Tom Williamson
Cyrus Wind Dancer
Lloyd Wolf
Sam Wynkoop

Thanks to Major Gene Duncan, USMC (Ret) for letting me quote from his book: *Fiction and Fact From Dunk's Almanac*, published by Gene Duncan, 715 6th Street, Boonville, MO 65233, copyright © 1980, and those fathers and sons who wished to remain anonymous, and those men from my childhood and life who have passed along the wisdom I have collected over the years. Their names have been forgotten, but the words remain.